Space Technology
NASA
Spinoffs
by Julie Murray
3
Dash!
LEVELED READERS
An Imprint of Abdo Zoom • abdobooks.com

Level 1 – Beginning
Short and simple sentences with familiar words or patterns for children who are beginning to understand how letters and sounds go together.

Level 2 – Emerging
Longer words and sentences with more complex language patterns for readers who are practicing common words and letter sounds.

Level 3 – Transitional
More developed language and vocabulary for readers who are becoming more independent.

abdobooks.com

Published by Abdo Zoom, a division of ABDO, PO Box 398166, Minneapolis, Minnesota 55439.

Printed in the United States of America, North Mankato, Minnesota.
102019
012020

Photo Credits: Alamy, iStock, NASA, Science Sourse, Shutterstock
Production Contributors: Kenny Abdo, Jennie Forsberg, Grace Hansen, John Hansen
Design Contributors: Dorothy Toth, Neil Klinepier, Victoria Bates

Library of Congress Control Number: 2019941326

Publisher's Cataloging in Publication Data

Names: Murray, Julie, author.
Title: NASA spinoffs / by Julie Murray
Description: Minneapolis, Minnesota : Abdo Zoom, 2020 | Series: Space technology | Includes online resources and index.
Identifiers: ISBN 9781532129261 (lib. bdg.) | ISBN 9781098220242 (ebook) | ISBN 9781098220730 (Read-to-Me ebook)
Subjects: LCSH: United States. National Aeronautics and Space Administration--Juvenile literature. | Space technology spinoffs--Juvenile literature. | Space sciences--Juvenile literature. | Technology transfer--Juvenile literature. | Technological innovations--Juvenile literature.
Classification: DDC 629.47--dc23

Table of Contents

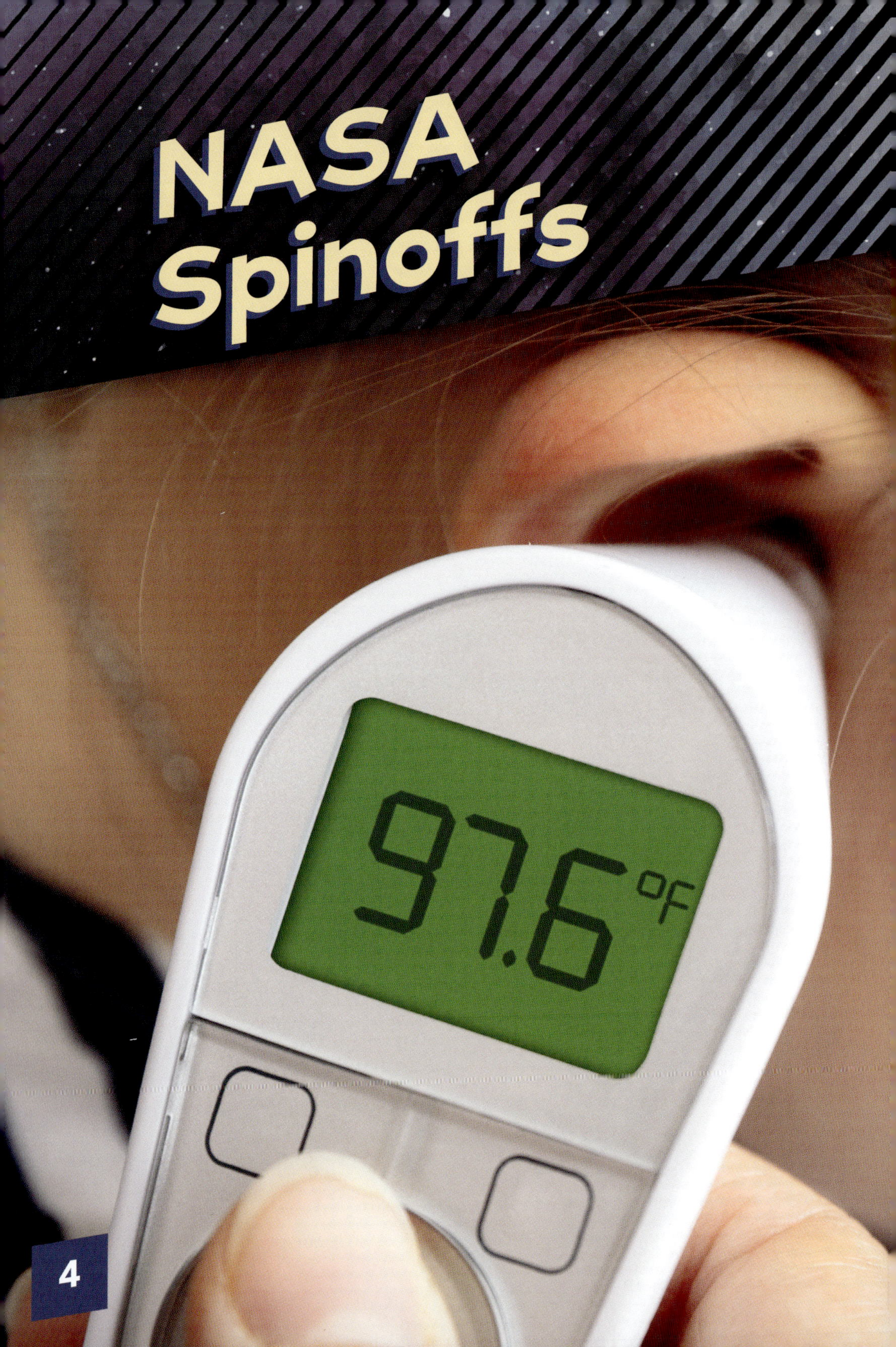

NASA Spinoffs

Have you ever used an ear thermometer? If so, you have used a NASA **spinoff**. NASA spinoffs are products made using NASA's technology or **research**.

What is NASA?

NASA stands for the National Aeronautics and Space Administration. It is a US government agency. NASA's mission is to explore space and flight.

Memory foam was designed by NASA-**funded researchers**. It was used to keep pilots comfortable while flying. Today, it is used in mattresses, cushions, and even shoes!

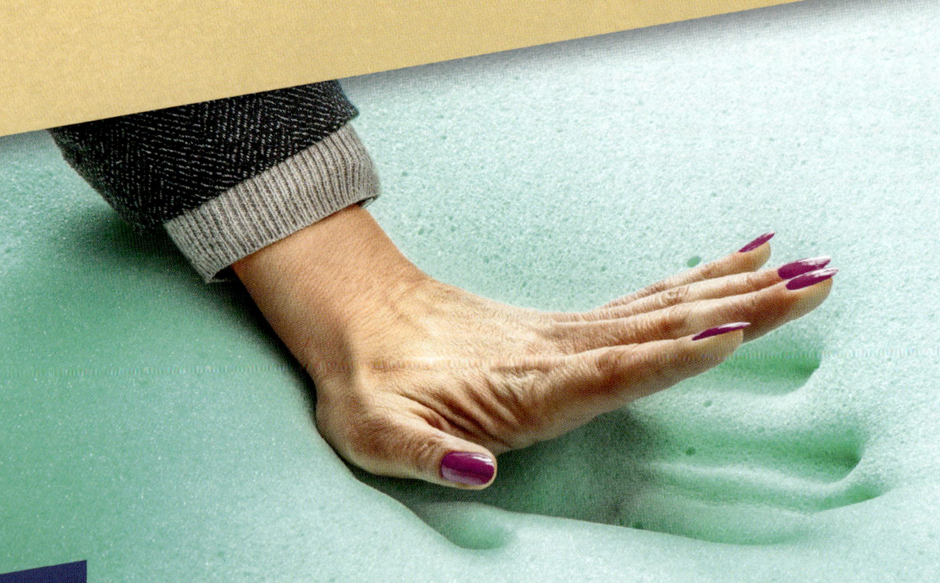

Wireless headsets use NASA technology. This is how Buzz Aldrin communicated from the Moon! Today, video game headsets use this technology too.

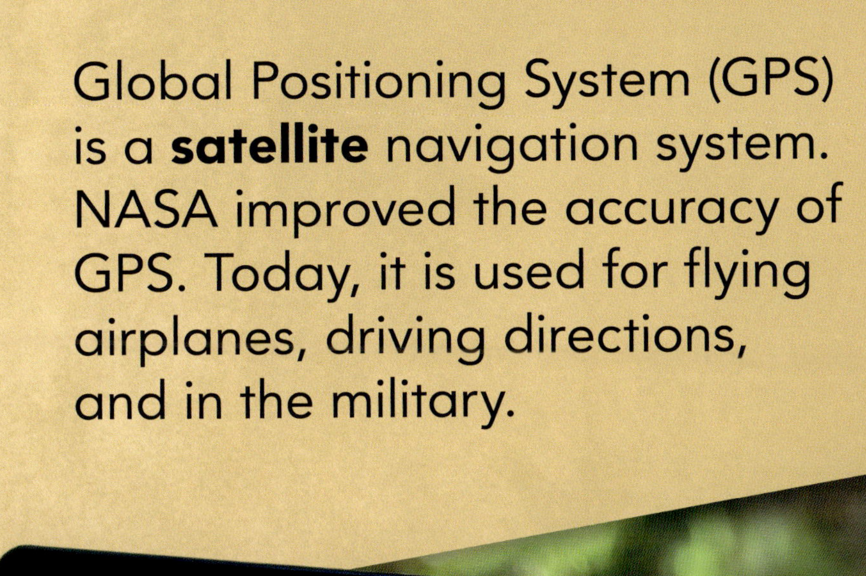

Global Positioning System (GPS) is a **satellite** navigation system. NASA improved the accuracy of GPS. Today, it is used for flying airplanes, driving directions, and in the military.

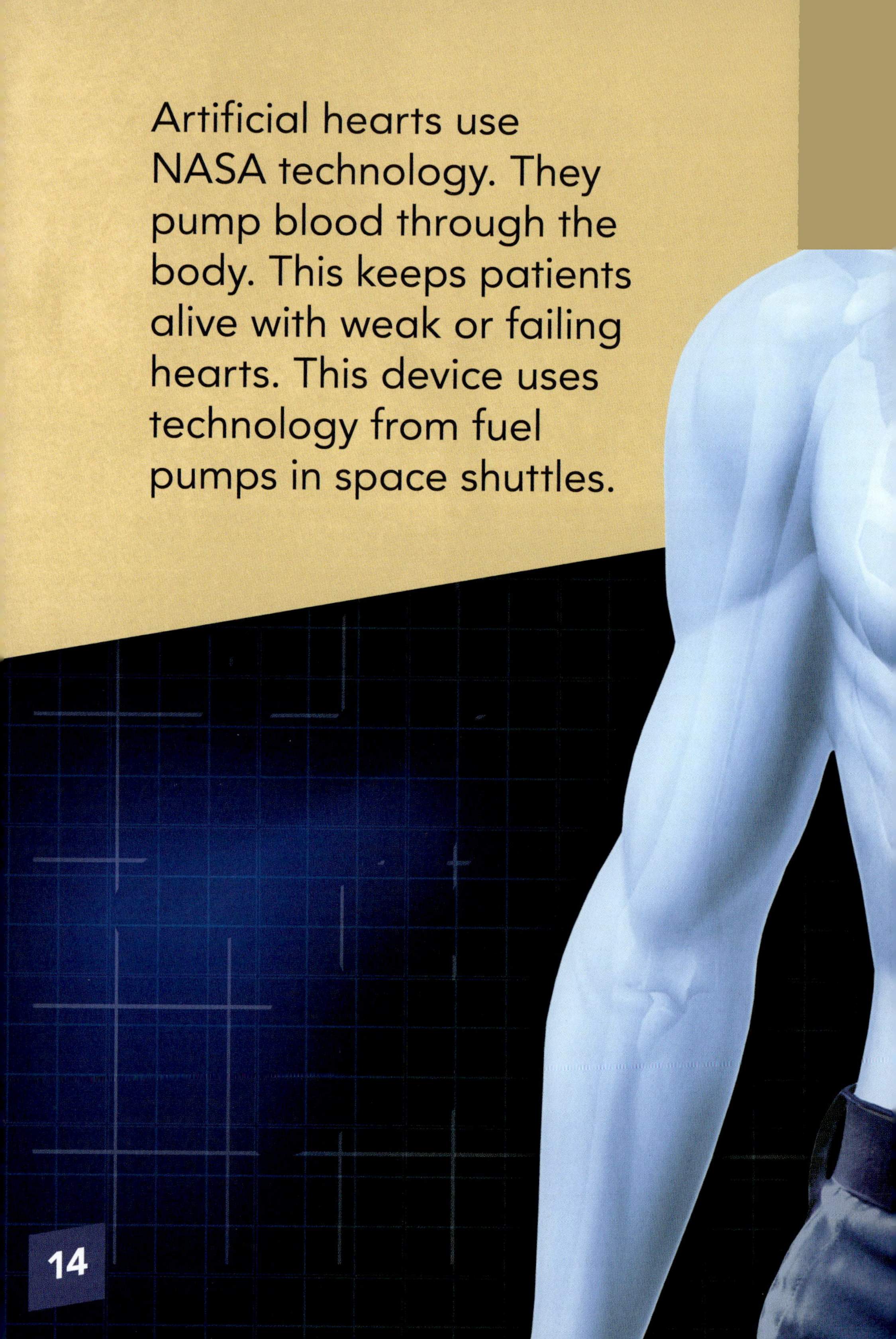

Artificial hearts use NASA technology. They pump blood through the body. This keeps patients alive with weak or failing hearts. This device uses technology from fuel pumps in space shuttles.

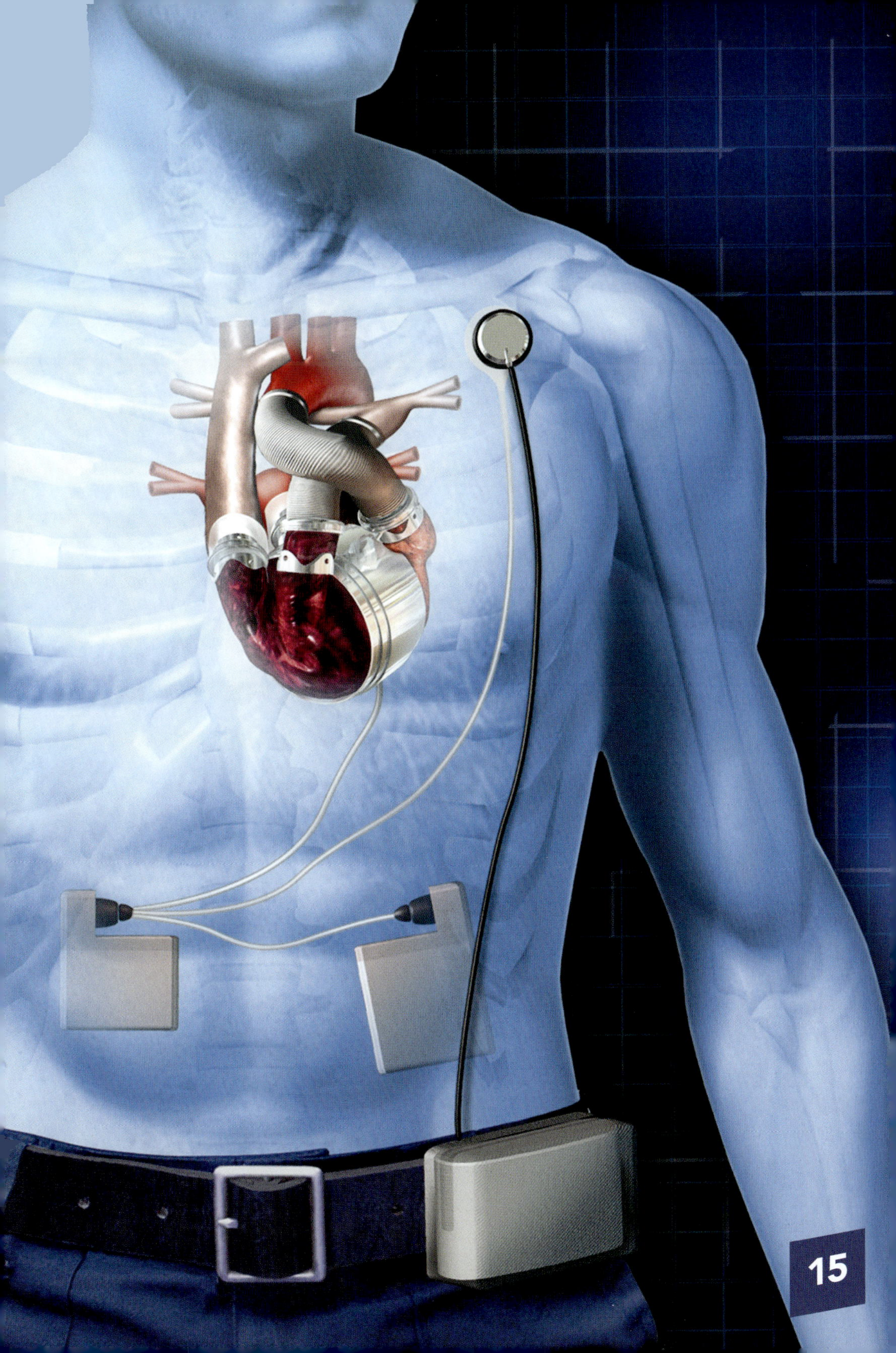

Freeze dried food was made for long missions to space. It is lightweight and **nutritious**. Today, it is used in the military. People also use it on camping trips.

Milk
Milk
5 OZ (21g)
EEDLESS GRAPES

Winglets use NASA technology. They reduce drag on an aircraft, helping save fuel. They also lower CO_2 emissions. Today, they are used on many airplanes.

Look around! Many things you see and use today are NASA **spinoffs**. These products improve the lives of millions of people each day.

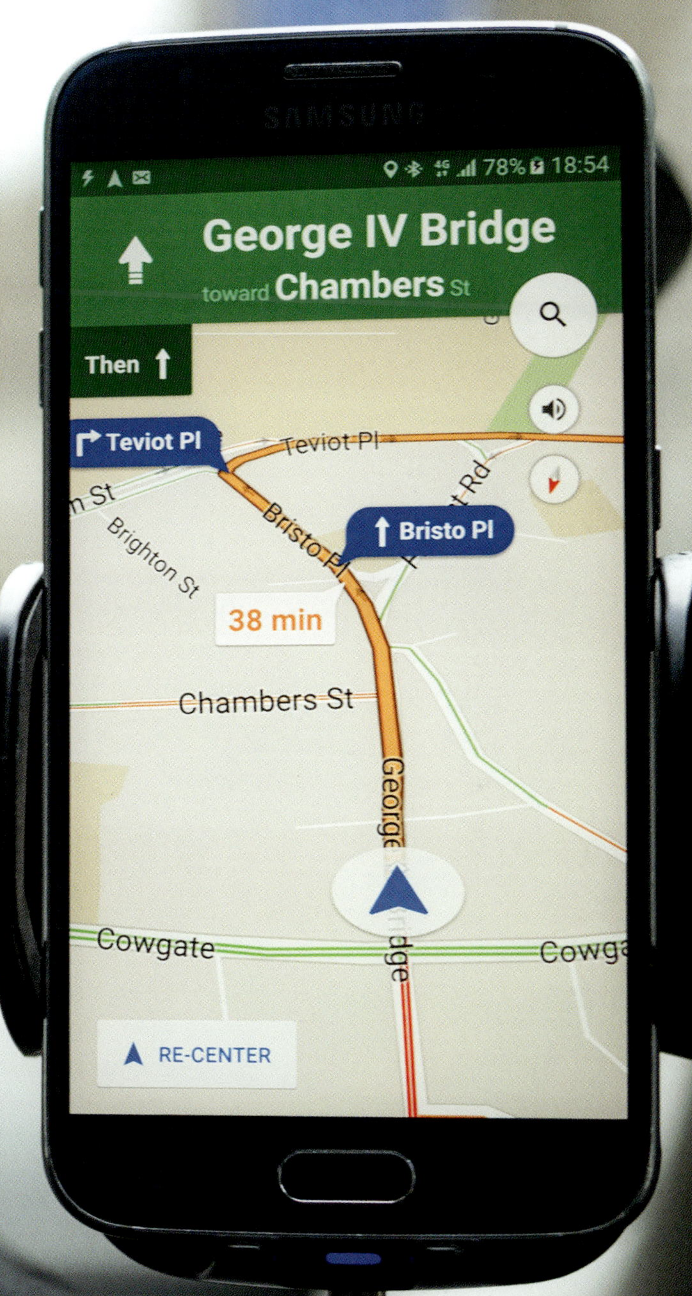
SAMSUNG
78% 18:54
George IV Bridge
toward Chambers St
Then
Teviot Pl
Teviot Pl
Bristo Pl
Bristo Pl
Brighton St
38 min
Chambers St
George
Cowgate
RE-CENTER

More NASA Spinoffs

- Air Purifier
- CAT Scan
- DUSTBUSTER® Vacuum
- Invisible Braces
- LED Lights
- Water Filter

Glossary

funded – provided money to pay for something.

nutritious – having a large amount of vitamins, minerals, or other nutrients.

research – careful study of something in order to find out information about it.

satellite – a man-made device placed in orbit around the earth or moon or another planet in order to collect information or for communication.

spinoff – something that comes into being as the result of the creation of other products.

Index

Online Resources

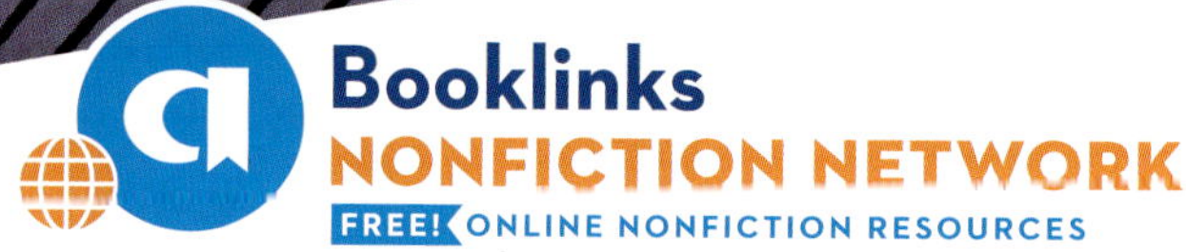

To learn more about NASA spinoffs, please visit **abdobooklinks.com** or scan this QR code. These links are routinely monitored and updated to provide the most current information available.